Mound Bayou, Mississippi

Mound Bayou, Mississippi was founded by Indigenous,

- (formerly: Colored, or Negro, or Black Person, African American)

businessmen in 1887 in Bolivar County.

Isaiah T. Montgomery,

Joshua P. T. Montgomery along with

Benjamin T. Green,

founded this town and populated it with their extended families and other productive Indigenous citizens to have a safe and peaceful place to raise families and thrive in a supportive business economy.

Moun' Bah 'oh

Table of Contents

Moun' Bah 'oh

Moun' Bah 'oh

Artificial Intelligence created all photos.

Moun' Bah 'oh

My Mound Bayou, Mississippi in 1967

In the year 1967 we moved to Mound Bayou Mississippi, from Boston, Massachusetts.

As we rode into town we slowed to a stop. A man spoke to my father.

"I see you brought your family! Well, welcome to Moun' Bah' Oh."

Our station wagon was parallel parked onto a sandy parking space between the sidewalk and Main Street, in front of our

new place to live. It was September and very warm walking into the tiny house already furnished. Up the three cement steps we walked onto a small landing with my father holding the glass storm door open for us. I walked into the living room happy to be out of the car and leaned against a woven brown couch. It had little golden threads in it if you looked close enough. I rubbed it, I smelled it (no smell) and looked around the house some more.

Under my feet was that large oval throw rug that many houses had (burgundy, blue, brown, and cream braided yarn stitched together). There were windows across from the couch, a desk under the windowsill and a chair to the left of that. My mother showed us the two bedrooms.

The Boston house had three floors and a basement and rooms everywhere. This house was not as big as our Boston house' first floor. We found our way around the house quickly.

There was a small front yard with high hedges all around and a screened in porch on the back of the house. The back yard was shady, wide, and lengthy, growing grass, plants, and trees. Pecan trees, peach, apple, and a mimosa tree with pink flowers. The yard had birds, worms, and bugs and a white shed we never went into. Me and my brother did our best to climb the apple tree, but we were so small we may have climbed only two feet off the ground that day, happily. The feeling of being in that back yard was wonderful. We had an alley behind our Boston house and no grass anywhere. Here, we did not have to walk to the park anymore.

On one side of the yard was a wire fence where you could see through the fence into the next yard. Right beside our house on the other side of the hedges was the house my new girls lived in. They had a faucet coming out of the ground beside their front door with a big round tin tub under the faucet. Their back yard was as long as ours with a path that went to a gravel road just like ours did. On the other side of my girls' yard was Mrs. Clary's yard with exceptionally large chicken coops and at least fifty loud chickens.

The next day we had breakfast in our teeny-weeny kitchen. The slim kitchen table was for a typewriter, it was white lacquer with that Black boarder stripe. Only three of us could sit there. Me, Bob, and Allan ate first, and Ma stood up getting us things.

After breakfast I went outside into the front yard.

I heard the girls next door walking and could see their dresses and legs moving on the other side of the hedges. I felt blocked, that I did not know them.

They looked different from the girls next door in Boston. It was a bunch of them like my bunch of Boston girls of various sizes.

I wanted to watch the Boston girls jump rope Double Dutch style again.

Moun' Bah 'oh

Ma said, 'say Hi!'. I sat on the sidewalk looking around and
across Main Street to the Railroad tracks, sadly experiencing
3-year-old stress! One of the girls came to where I was
sitting and asked my name. She then pulled Binky in front of
her and said, "This is the one you can play with, she is your
size."

Moun' Bah 'oh

Our New Telephone

Our new telephone number was 3-4. Just a number 3 and a number 4. Nice and easy to remember. Any time you picked up the telephone, a lady who was the Operator would say, "Mound Bayou: You paid?", Mr. Huddleston owned the phone company.

The First Night in 1967 Mississippi I was sick.

Being sick in the daytime in Mississippi back then was DANGEROUS! and here I go with some type of condition at night, where Ma was saying to Pa, "Are there any stores open? All we need to get for her is _____ if we get it tonight then she will be better in the morning.

Before traveling anywhere in the south, "Black" people had to consider the many notorious and tragic incidents that occurred.

At the time we moved to Mound Bayou, twelve scary violent years had passed since Carolyn Bryant allegedly participated in getting Emmett Till, killed (1955). Three years since Byron De La Beckwith assassinated Medgar Evers (1963). Mr. Evers had lived and worked in Mound Bayou.

In about 1964, Eighteen members of the Ku Klux Klan were charged for killing the three men from CORE (Congress of Racial Equity); James Chaney, Andrew Goodman, and Michael Schwerner. I remember seeing the news in 1967 when the federal trial was going on. Their three photos were on tv. The news showed the dam where their bodies were discovered.

"They killed those young fellas", Ma said sadly, as we watched the news.

Soon, was Martin Luther King's assassination.

On the smooth part of the wall in my first-grade classroom there was a calendar with Martin Luther King's portrait. It was April 1968: Sister Mary, our first-grade teacher, wanted us to look at the photo of Martin Luther King and focus intently on his facial details to draw his picture. She was praising him, honoring him, and touching the photo while describing his facial features so we could do our best to create a great drawing.

She passed out manila colored paper to all of us and a black fat pencil to use. My drawing was going to be the best because I knew him, and he was great, and I could not wait to begin my masterpiece. I had the waves in his hair drawn right! I had the flare of his nostrils correct! And his lips were like a heart to me so that is what I drew perfectly. That is him! That was him on my paper doggone it! I did not have a crayon the same color as him, brown like my dad, and brown like Father Guidry. (We did not have any crayons at school). Within that same week, Martin Luther King was killed, to my horror and the horror of my first-grade class and everyone in Mound Bayou. The next day we got to school; Sister Mary was distraught, pacing the floor, trying to explain it to us all. It was a sickening feeling. My little six-year-old self was jolted! As if he was snatch off my paper, off my desk and balled up! Gone!

The Calendar remained up on the wall above the wood paneling, but now the picture was different from when we drew him. The whole tone and atmosphere changed when I looked at him every day after that. The page with the month of April 1968 with this picture, did not change until the month of May, to another him, in another pose, doing something else.

Soon, on our little 13-inch TV in the living room, the news was showing his funeral, with close ups of his daughters dressed nicely wearing ponytails like girls in my class, shiny curls with bows. I remember his casket and the horses pulling the carriage and the sadness. My family loved him. Ma knew Malcolm X in Boston, but we did not talk about him at home yet.

I heard my father talking about Martin Luther King my whole little life. In Boston, Pa and my brother Allan had marched with Martin and Stokely Carmichael (another famous activist), around the time I was born. Allan did not really march because he was two years old, so Pa marched with him on his shoulders.

Ma had deep feelings and doubt about leaving Boston and moving to Mississippi because of the meanness and danger that was probable, or definite. Going to the South was one thing but Mississippi was another! MISSISSIPPI dear reader, WAS A! NOTHER! In those times.

Ma had been a secretary at the, Harriet Tubman Alms House in Boston when she met Pa. Her secretarial career started at the Pentagon in Washington, D.C. right after she graduated from secretarial school. She was an expert typist and tele-typist. She   taught about office work, and how to write business letters at Tufts Delta Health Center.

Mound Bayou, Mississippi was selected by my father and his professional colleagues because it was an all-Black incorporated town where Black people and White people could have meetings together and plan the health center details without getting in legal trouble. They didn't want to be harassed by officers or jailed or killed. One time health center staff had a meeting, all jammed up on a school bus to maintain secrecy.

There were professionals of all race's cultures and backgrounds:

engineers, dentists: (We had a friend whose dad was a dentist and every time our friend lost a tooth his dad made him a partial with a false tooth to fill that space.) We had sanitation experts, environmental experts to manage mosquitos and extermination of other bugs. There were sewage and household safety professionals, home builders, farmers from big companies like the Bird's Eye company. Bird's Eye engineers had meetings to help the community and professionals manage the huge crops, crop collection and storage.

Our St. Gabriel School Nuns were all Black but there was one, our principal that was a white skinned lady, but she was 'Black', so they say, and that was confusing. The Nuns I saw at Tuft's Delta health center were white skinned like her, with other occupations like nun/nurses and nun/social workers, and nun/doctors.

The energy of us moving to Moun' Bah' oh and the health center project was great. My parents were excited to be there.

Moun' Bah 'oh

Now, let us go back and finish with my sickness.

I needed a medicine in 1967 Mississippi. The brothers were asleep, but I got up and my parents were awake and still talking with a lamp on in the living room. We did not have the medicine I needed, and I remember sitting down in there with them. It was dark and NIGHTTIME in Mississippi. Mound Bayou had no stores open. Ten miles away, Cleveland, Mississippi is a larger town with many stores, so maybe a store is open this night. Ma said all Leah needs is ____ (Whatever it was). They chatted a while about making that trip on the dark roads. Pa took a breath and looked at Ma and then looked at me, and

Moun' Bah 'oh

said, "Let's go."

 We found a large grocery store in Cleveland, Mississippi, and me and Ma got out of the car. One older heavy set white man was at the entrance of the store, looking down at papers on his counter, he nodded when we walked in, and my mother said 'Hello.'

There were six empty cash registers or more that we passed. 'I just need some medicine for her'. We are walking quickly! Cutting between the registers. Ma's high heels clicking with her skirt and stockings making swishing sounds, and my Mary Jane shoes clicking twice as fast. Mind you now, there is urgency to hurry up(!) to get out of the store and there is urgency to medicate me (!) there is urgency to make it home(!) 10 miles (!) in the dark night. We went down the aisle and Ma finds the medicine and grabs it quickly. Ma was relieved, I felt relieved also and then we heard a voice. A white lady's voice with a southern accent greeting the same man happily, seemingly in a hurry also. I hear her heels clicking hard on the floor like ours. Here she comes up our same aisle. Why the same aisle? In this huge place? We were trying to do all this undetected. I was afraid.

In the store, Ma has my left hand with her right hand, the lady is passing on Ma's left and in a split second, I twisted behind Ma still holding her hand and kicked the woman on her leg before she could do anything to us. My civil rights fight had begun!

Ma said, Oh! What did you do?! 'Oh my, we are sorry!'. We swished and clicked faster, passing the man on the way out. Ma put a large bill down and did not wait for any change. She lifted me up with by one arm swiftly making it to the exit. Only one of my Mary Janes was clicking at this point, while the lady was walking quickly after us, clickity click, clickity click!

'That little girl kicked me! She kicked me!" Said the offended lady.

The man at the desk looked up and shrugged his shoulders and shook his head. She was screaming like she wanted him to crucify me. He shrugged his shoulders.

Well, I was in trouble. My civil rights fight had absolutely started at the wrong time. I had upset folks. Crucifixion was not exactly on Ma's mind, but her blood pressure went up surely.

Pa was in the car waiting as we hustled into it, he asked what happened and Ma said "Let's go, Go! Leah was kicking her feet around and kicked that woman. Pa hit the gas! We made it the ten miles home and my fellow soldiers made me go directly to bed after taking the medicine. There was no discussion about my valiant effort to help people of color in America that night. I could not even attempt to relax in the living room in the dim lighting with my fellow soldiers since I was in trouble. Even though Ma cured me with the medicine, she may have needed something for her state of shock. Tomorrow will be a better day.

Even though I was young I felt the seriousness of the civil rights movement. Many White people in Mississippi do not like us and are mean, was my interpretation. But! That was confusing too because we had white friends that were nice to us. Dr. Jack Geiger was a white color with a blue or yellow tint I noticed sometimes.

He was another important team member in planning and implementing the Mound Bayou Health center project. His wife

Moun' Bah 'oh

was white too but a different white color than his white color. She sat me in her lap at the meeting they had on the school bus and taught me how to tie my shoes. That was magical step up for me in life.

St Gabriel Catholic School

I remember my mother being excited to take me to the preschool class at Saint Gabriel Catholic School. I had not seen Ma as excited before. She was Catholic and Catholic was glorious to her. I did not think going to school was a glorious idea. What was on their minds because our new house is just fine? Gloriously taking me to school to gloriously leave me with strangers and a Nun that floated across the room with no legs, of which I was afraid. In my four-year-old opinion, Nope, Nuns did not have legs because nobody could see any legs. My entry into the class was quite loud with me crying all day.

The Nun, Sister Mary____, was a brown color and she moved fast back and forth across the front area of the room, speaking loudly while she taught. She used big movement and gestures when we all sang, or when she told us stories. I headed the line when we all went outside, or to the cafeteria because I was the shortest.

Father Guidry oversaw the school. He was brown just like my father and happy to see his students all the time.

All the kids liked to greet him and crowd around him. He

would   give a pat on the cheek to the students near him.

On the cover of the book, you can see me with our German
Shepard named Cheyenne. Cheyenne would sit in the front
yard protecting me and my brother as we played. One
morning as we were getting ready for school, we could not
find Cheyenne. My father went outside into the foggy air and
quickly came in and told us he was dead. Fear was what I felt
at that moment. Fear, fear, fear. Dead? Someone had
poisoned our Cheyenne. We wanted to see him. Pa said we
could not see him and got a sheet and wrapped him up to put
him in the back of the station wagon.

Moun' Bah 'oh

Ma and Pa said he was too scary looking for the people. I remember him barking and folks taking off running extremely fast from his loud barks. It surprised me that they were afraid because he was nice to us. From what the family says he worked for the Boston Police before we got him. Rest in Peace Cheyenne Hatch. Father Guidry had a German Shepard also killed around the same time.

German Shepards were employed by police departments to bite and scare people marching and protesting for civil rights. We missed him very much and wondered who gave him the poison.

The Cafeteria at St. Gabriel

As you walk into St. Gabriel School there was a door to the immediate left. That was the cafeteria which was amazing to me to only eat at a long table with so many kids.

There was a long bar with ladies behind it preparing our plates. It was hard to see the ladies because of the windows with bright light behind them. The plates had hills of food. I was not much of an eater and can only remember a pile of collard greens on my plate. One of my little classmates, happily splashed my plate with vinegar,

'You are supposed to put this on greens!' she said.

I said, "oh" and tasted it. I may as well have been sticking my finger in an electrical socket. The sour taste zapped my whole body. I did not taste greens again for many, many years.

Performances at school

At St. Gabriel we prepared for performances but most times we did not perform whatever we practiced. We rehearsed for a Pinocchio play. I was one of the 10 or 15 Jiminy Crickets and I had a speaking part.

At one point when school was out, there was another performance and practice. Two white ladies came from South Africa one summer and taught us songs to perform.

'We are marching to Pretoria, Pretoria Hurrah!', Ring around the Rosy, and a few other songs. We also had to hold a tinfoil holder with a rose in it. We had to sing, SHaaaaaaaaaah, while pushing the rose high to the sky! Which was hilarious to adults there. I did not know what 'shaaaaaah' meant but I and the other performers were serious about singing 'shaaaaaah'.

Ma dressed me up for the performance but was not dressed.

She was going to dress quickly and come in a few minutes. "Where is Allan? She spoke.

Moun' Bah 'oh

I said he is outside on his bike with B.B.

Ma told him to ride me to the program at school.

Allan put me on the back of his bike and told me, "Hold onto my shirt'. We rode 3 blocks to St. Gabriel.

Performers lined up in a circle. Allan was nearby sitting on his bike holding it up, as we sang the songs in about five minutes.

Allan, put me back on his bike, rode me back home. As we walked inside the house, Ma was in a dress and great high heeled shoes with perfume sprayed everywhere. She was in the bathroom, putting on her lipstick. Surprised to see us back so soon she asked,

"What happened?!"

Allan said,

 "They finished!"

Ma laughed hysterically, and in her New England accent said,

"It's ovuh?!"

I could not connect anything funny with this situation because, I practiced, I dressed up and sang beautifully and she didn't see it.

Days after this performance me and my father had a short conference in the station wagon. I was telling on Ma and how she did not get to see me sing. He said, 'ok well, sing the songs for me.' He was in the driver's seat, and I was behind him in the back seat.

I piped up singing," We are marching to Pretoria, Pretoria, Pretoria, we are marching to Pretoria Hurrah!"   Pa start

Moun' Bah 'oh

shaking his head saying 'No, no, no. What?! Who taught you that?

'Some ladies at school' I replied. He had a surprised reaction, shaking his head, saying I cannot believe

it! Who are these ladies?

I did not really know. Thinking back at the ladies' physical appearances; They were not dressed up like Ma or the other ladies in Mound Bayou with dresses and curled up hair and high heels. They had short hair, no make-up or lipstick, their clothes were plain, so they may have been nuns in training, visiting the convent at our catholic school.

In the country of South Africa and in its city of Pretoria, as was happening in America, was protesting, and killing of a lot of people. Nelson Mandela of the African National Congress was in jail over there a year or two by the time we got to Mound Bayou. My young self-singing about Pretoria was just not supposed to happen.

Back in the 1800's, allegedly, it was a song of comradery among British soldiers while marching together to fight the Dutch already established in South Africa. Brittain had a plan to own all of Africa. Meanwhile the South African, Indigenous people with dark skin were more than oppressed. So, the last part of that station wagon conference was, 'You are not marching to Pretoria.'

 I recall another station wagon conference with my father
when he just had to take something somewhere or he was
going to another meeting he could bring kids to. There was
always something on the backseat, files, papers with
envelopes in a box or something. This time under my feet on
the floorboard was a poster. It had a photo of an African
teenager of about 15 years. I was trying to read it. I knew
one word was from a gas station we use to stop at sometimes.
It was in orange writing and the other word was Boycott. I
could read the 'Boy' letters of the word. Who is this boy, Pa?
and what is this other word, his name? He explained it all.
What a boycott was and how Gulf was not paying the
people enough to live off and was taking oil from the land
and making millions of dollars off the poor people. So, if we
get people to stop buying that type of gas then maybe they
will either pay the African people more money or leave their
land and country alone.

The Co-Op and the Corn Field.

Here are what the trailers looked like beside the health center, which were for teaching health classes.

Moun' Bah 'oh

(Circa 2010) I met a nurse from a plantation hospital near Cleveland Mississippi, who was visiting her mother, a patient of mine North Carolina. I mentioned living near Cleveland and Tuft's Delta Health Center. She paused and seemed a bit startled while feeding her mother. She said, "That was YOUR dad? 'The Delta health center was the best thing that happened to that area prior to Medicaid."

Moun' Bah 'oh

One thing the health center had was crops. Crops, crops and more crops. Corn, string beans, tomatoes, and all sorts of vegetables to improve the health of all the citizens.

Neighborhood groups would take turns planting and harvesting. In the summertime we would see buses with grown people wearing heavy winter coats and scarves and hats riding into the fields. Sweating in those clothes kept them cool and protected skin from insects and from the sun. Me and my brothers visited the fields to see the string bean vines, corn on the stalks, peas, and okra and more.

On a hot evening as the sun was going down, Pa drives home on a pickup truck from the CO-OP.

 "Let's go for a ride!" We were excited. We rode towards the town of Marigold, to a CO-OP corn field across from Reverend Daniel's large farm. In the corn field Pa put me and Allan in the bed of the truck to give us a 'fun ride.' Pa drove and bounced the truck around, until ow! And ow! we hit all parts of the bed of the truck, bouncing like a boat in the ocean. Suddenly and thankfully the truck was stuck in the mud. We all got out of the truck and Pa spun the tires flinging the mud chunks and water everywhere. The truck was stuck.

Moun' Bah 'oh

The sun was just now leaving the sky at the same time we trudged through the corn rows. We made it to the road and spent time wiping the mud off.

My Mary Jane shoes were muddy brown, no longer red. It was dark and how would we get home? I would love to tell you of the discussion between my parents at this point but, go ahead and imagine. We began to walk to Mound Ba' oh,' past Reverend Daniel's farm, past his beautiful brick home.

Moun' Bah 'oh

Here come car lights toward us, also headed towards Moun' Bah 'oh. The man slowed his car down looking in amazement at my muddy family walking on the highway. My father knew him and walked to his window to get us a ride. As we piled into his car, he looked at each one of us strangely.

The Flood

One morning we woke up and I could hear water. Cars riding through water. The Mississippi river had flooded our new town. The water was soaking our yard, touching the house, covering the first step of the three. I just thought this is wonderful. Water was everywhere, we liked water and wanted to go outside. "No" was the answer of course so we just stood at the door and watched the water moving all around. My father was always busy, so we watched him leave again wearing rain boots as he sloshed down the walkway to the car. We wanted to slosh. When the car moved the water spun off the tires. That was the absolute greatest.

Fishing

I learned to fish and use a fishing rod at 4 years old. I always wanted to go fishing.

We went on a boat sometimes taking cane poles and one fancy rod with a reel. I watched closely as Pa used the rod with the reel. I would say, 'I can do it. Pa, can I do it? Please let me.

"No, not this one, you might drop it in the water. "

So finally, one fishing day he said yes! He rowed us close to the shore in case he had to get it out of the water. I did it with no problem, so smoothly. I did not catch anything during that trip, but I could cast with a rod and reel.

There was a little lake equal to the size of two football fields beside the health center.

My younger brother had a fishing stick with fishing line and a bobber on the line with worms on the hook.

Moun' Bah 'oh

At the lake he would walk to the small pier or go sit on the grass on the bank. When he put his hook into the water,

the fish would swarm the bait. He was still 3 years old.

Allan was always doing bigger fishing than us. He could walk to places we could not reach like logs and in bushes. Sometimes Allan caught bigger fish than Pa would catch.

On this momentous day, Pa casted a line out far and let me hold the pole giving specific directions on how to manage my fishing situation.

"Do not reel it in until you feel the fish pulling, ok?"

'OK.' So yes, I had my assignment standing there on the high bank of the lake, with rod and reel in both hands, waiting for my gigantic fish. A lady that was fishing near us was looking at me and said to everyone, 'That baby can't do nothing. You ain't gone catch nothing baby."

What a kind voice she had, but offended I was by her negative words. She insulted my beautiful fishing abilities. Her words were just preposterous!

Now, on with the legend.

Suddenly folks, the pole jerked twice. Pa had walked away already, and I began to reel MY fish in. I shouted at the top of my lungs for the lady and all of Mound Bayou to hear,

 'I got one, I got a fish!"

The lady said. "You ain't got nothing but MOSS!"

I knew she was wrong, and she would be as shocked as everyone else on that beautiful sun shiny day!

I was winding the reel and then I could not wind it. I screamed!

 'Pa! I got one!

Pa turned and saw the tip of the pole curved severely towards the

water! My monster of a fish was pulling. Trying to pull me in the lake

and have me for dinner. But no! Pa ran over to check it and found the fish

was fighting like Joe Frazier! Pa was laughing loudly, fighting back like

Muhammed Ali. He pulled my monster fish out of the water. What a beautiful gigantic fish sparkling and wiggling for all to see! The legend is

that it was a about a 3-pound bass.

 The lady was shocked and said,
"Well, I guess I will get me one of those fancy rods."

Easter Shoes

We were getting ready for an Easter program at church and my younger brother was having a fit because he did not want to wear his new leather shoes. My parents wrestled with his feet, explained the importance of church attire, hard shoes go with a new suit; they begged him, they tried to bribe him with a match box car. Back and forth! "No! was his stance. Ma got tired, then, Pa was also tired of wrestling those legs and feet with balled up toes. They let him wear his new sneakers. I went into shock.

It was time to go to church and we had to bring in this non-conformist with P.F. Flyers on his feet (sneakers made him run faster and jump higher, of course). I just knew it was over for all of us. The Reverend and everyone would make us go back home because of the sneakers. We made it to the church parking lot, and I was afraid, looking at the adults faces. Waiting to see when our moment of rejection would come. Ma and Pa had on their, meeting and greeting faces, saying hello to other people that were also getting out of their cars. We made it to the front door of the church, and not one person said a thing, no one noticed. He was before his time.

My Bike

I had a set of training wheels. I bugged Pa to put them on my new purple bike, but he did not get a chance to. I would go look at my training wheels from time to time in the bottom drawer of his dresser knowing one day I will be riding smoothly like Allan. So, on my bike I would just try and balance, hit a peddle and wiggle, and catch myself, leaning on one side or the other, while Ma rode her bike on the sidewalk. On nice nights, the street was full of people talking, walking, kids playing. One evening I did it! I learned to ride without training wheels.

Moun' Bah 'oh

Mrs. Clary

Mrs. Clary was our neighbor with the chicken coops. She had a restaurant in her kitchen with three tables and a refrigerator with all kinds of soda pops for sale. She was a large woman with a slim husband and always wore a smile on her face and an apron on her dress. Her hair usually was decorated with a scarf. If Ma's little hands could not open a jar or bottle, Ma would send me to Mrs. Clary's house with the jar for her to open for us. We would buy two coca-colas to go with dinner sometimes.

Moun' Bah 'oh

The new brown paper bags Miss Clary would put the cokes in, smelled like cigarette smoke and the tasty food she cooked.

What we have learned since leaving Mound Bayou, is that Mound Bayou is on the Historic Chitlin Circuit. It was a safe place for Black/Indigenous artists to perform. Mrs. Clary cooked for musicians and other performers and party goers because we had night clubs in Mound Bayou. If kids stayed out until dusk, we would see people coming to town with shiny cars, sharp suits on, wearing shiny shoes pretty dresses and matching hats.

I was next door at Sindie's house one of these evenings with the girls playing in the dirt. We watched Mrs. Clary come out

in her yard with a knife by her side catching our full attention.
Sindie said 'Ooh, there she goes!'

Mrs. Clary had come out to get a chicken. She would lean
forward and run towards a chicken, raising her knife, and
swinging it at the chicken.

The assaulted chicken would still run all around all hurt until
she grabbed its feet, taking it in her back door. The other
chickens would run and scream and cluck and make gobbling

sounds. It would take a while for the other chickens to settle down after something like that (just like people). When the chicken's calmed down we would catch our breath too and start playing in the dirt again.

Binky's House and the Soldier

Binky and I would play around the yard often and she and her sisters would come around the hedges to my birthday parties sometimes. I usually went around the hedges over her house in the back yard.

Binky's Uncle had a big house. Uncle lived in the front of the house and Madea; Uncle's niece, lived in the back of the house with her daughters. On another day I went over there and Binky said, "My Daddy here." I was happy to see him. "There go my Daddy right there.", Out steps a United States soldier in a green starched and pressed uniform with his face looking just like Binky. 'Do you want some money, Leah?' Binky said. Da' will give you some money.' I was silent, just staring, taking it all in. A real live soldier! Binky's father is a real live soldier. Da' was a soldier from Vietnam. On our coffee table we had magazines, Newsweek, Time, and the National Geographic. Sometimes the magazines had scenes of smoky, Vietnam showing people running in the smoke and soldiers dressed like Da.' A real live soldier! Da' squatted down to our level and pulled out a shiny quarter and gave it to me. Money!

(I could buy about fifty pieces of candy with that quarter.) He stood up, picking Binky up while giving her hugs and kisses. Da' had a soldier bag on the ground. He put her down and then picked up the bag and walked away on the path by the hedges.

Moun' Bah 'oh

Our Other Neighbors

This gentleman lived a few doors down from us. Information from the Epsilon Xi Lambda Chapter of Alpha Phi Alpha website says, Fred Miller was the president of Alpha Phi

Alpha Fraternity Inc. from 1911 to 1912. Ma said he was about 70 years old when he asked her to dance at one of the parties held at the recreation center. We would see him always dressed up and going places. Walking into his house fast. Walking to his car fast and waving at passersby. He had extra rooms in his house and sometimes people visiting the health center could stay there for a brief time.

Right next door was a hairdresser in a large red house. I got to go in there once and saw her doing someone's hair.

I saw people go in and come out with new, Easter hair, and Christmas hair and Church hair.

Music, Dancing and Michael Jackson

Well folks, I loved to dance the latest and the greatest dances of the 1960's. I learned dances over GG's house. GG was 9 years old with two younger brothers BB and Junior, both brothers could do the 'James Brown' dance wiggling and sliding their feet on the floor. The James Brown split was a difficult skill to learn and maneuver but they could do it so easily. The other dances we learned had names like; The Popcorn, The 'Funky, Funky Broadway', The Boogaloo, The Funky Chicken.   We could do them all.

(Add Hula dancing to the list too. I learned Hula because one of the store owners in town had a wife from Hawaii that came to the school and taught us Ha Ta Po Po.)

Moun' Bah 'oh

My big friend GG became our 'manager'. Her smallest
brother Junior, five years old, was my dance contest partner
when I was six.

We had fun practicing our dances in their car port. Junior and I won about four dance contests against 'big people' (adults) and older children.

Ma would get me ready to go out with GG. The little crowd of kids would come down the sidewalk to our house and collect me. Once we got to our venue, my people, GG, would talk to 'their people," at the school auditorium or a party and get information on our time to get on stage and do our dancing. When we would get on the stage to dance, GG would stand in the audience telling Junior and I which dances to switch to.

We became rich after a contest, winning twelve dollars. The money was embezzled by one of the older taller "promoters."

The professionals coming from all over the United States often brought kids. One day we visited Ed's house, a community organizer from Boston. His children, Brenda and Michael were upstairs playing records and singing. We could hear them as we went upstairs. They were sitting on their beds singing, snapping their fingers to the music. They did not say hello until they finished singing. What an event! They could snap and pop their fingers and sing at the same time! I could not snap mine at all!

The music sounded heavenly, and I wanted to know the words like Brenda sang them! It was the Jackson 5.

The record player screamed!

"Stop! You better save me!....... and the next record was, ABC! Easy as 123! I could relate! Being in the first grade, this information was part of my curriculum, and Ma called money; dough re me! So, I knew all the words! Brenda played the records over and over, repeatedly. The lead singer sounded like a kid! I wondered how a kid could be on that record?! How? When it was time to leave, I just was not ready to go. I wanted to hear more. Having to leave that great music in that moment was a total injustice. Pa had to use a loud voice to make us leave, coming up the stairs to get us. He carried us out sideways like luggage. We did not have music at our house, like that. It was great!

Tina Turner and Tom Jones were who Ma liked.

She would sit on a chair in front of our 10-inch TV and clap her hands and move her shoulders. That is as close to dancing as I saw her do. Tina Turner was superior, in a league of her own on the television.

Other shows I recall watching in those days were, Jack LaLane's Exercise after the morning news, Bozo the clown, Betty Boop and Dark Shadows, Marcus Wellby MD, In like Flint, and Julia. Tom Jones came on every Sunday and Ma was ready!

Quite Noticeable

It must have been about dinner time because the sun was behind our house on Main Street. It was shining through the trees making shadows on main street. Shining brightly on the railroad tracks and on the business buildings across the tracks too. Me and Ma were riding our bikes on our sidewalk when a nicely dressed lady was walking by and stopped to talk to Ma. She was shaking her head and looking at Kay about fifteen yards away. Kay was standing in the street in front of the hairdresser's red house. I looked at Kay and saw her laughing and talking with kids. Girls did not wear pants much, back then, but Kay dressed just like boys.

Still shaking her head and looking concerned, the lady said, "I wish her parents would tell her to quit walking around by herself." Ma glanced over at Kay and said to the lady "Yes" I have seen her walking around in the street and on the railroad tracks a time or two."

I did not know what would happen to her or what the lady was afraid of either. Seeing a white girl walk around Mound Bayou was odd; something you never see.

Ms. Pearly B.

Visiting Miss Pearly B was another mission we got to go on with my father.

Ms. Pearly B. was a local wonder woman type that lived in the nearby town of Round Lake, Mississippi.

My parents have so many good stories about her feats of greatness.

Her house was dark, nice, and neat as I looked around while she and my father talked. I needed a bathroom and asked Ms. Pearly B. She walked me to the back door and opened it while pointing over to her out house (outside toilet). It was about thirty feet from her back door. I thought a porcelain toilet would be on the other side of the door, not air, and sky, and yard. As she was shaking her head and mumbling about me, "She ain't gone use it." (my thought was 'you're right') then she switched to a louder voice and said,

'Let me show you how it looks inside.' We went and looked and nope! I was not going in, never had I seen anything like it. It was not something I could do. I was just going to hold it.

Ms. Pearly B. said,

"John she isn't going in there!"

I held 'it' strongly, and at that same time ants were attacking my brother as he played on the ground, so it was time to go.

"There is a gas station down the road with a white man in it" that might let me relieve myself she told us. Pa and Ms. Pearly B. shook the ants off brother, said goodbye. We zipped down the road to the white man that let me in to use the bathroom.

Pearly B. was key in helping the people of Bolivar County. She knew the culture and needs of the people. She suggested builders add steps to people's homes to make it easier for old people and pregnant women to get into their houses. They added screens to windows to prevent insects from entering, especially mosquitos that transmitted encephalitis. She helped pregnant women to get other the things they needed. Senior citizens were a focus as many of their able-bodied relatives would move to Chicago and other cities for jobs. She was put in charge of Senior services at the health center and did an amazing job there.

Pearly B. would tell my parents stories of events in her life. She told them around the start of WWII (1939), she was working in a cotton field picking cotton. One day while working, she was calculating the money she had earned in her first three hours of that day. The amount was less than a dollar in total, and suddenly she heard God's deep voice say, "Pearly B., pick no more!" She threw down her garden hoe and left to go plan and start her new business.

The Lock

The lock on the church, was another story significant to social and civil rights history in Bolivar County.

 Mrs. Pearly B. and her husband would donate their time helping to keep the church clean and repaired. One day they went to take care of the church and found an extra lock on the doors. They went and asked the pastor why he put the extra lock on the church. His response was that he did not want any Black and White radical health center people having meetings together... bringing trouble to him and his church. Pearlie B.'s point of view was that the meetings were helping people that attended the church and helping the community, and White people and Black people needed a place to meet. So, no one was getting in. Not even the pastor as she put a lock on top of his lock. Later they agreed to have a meeting to solve the discrepancies and eventually they held a grand ceremony with prayer and a meal to unlock both locks civilly, and peacefully.

For people of the community and migrants coming through that worked in cotton fields, Pearlie B. suggested to the plantation owner to let the workers plant a row of food beside the cotton so they would have something to eat when they wanted. The owner agreed.

The Census Taker

My younger brother and I were playing in the front yard one day. A tall skinny young white fellow in a black skinny suit, with a white shirt and skinny tie, was stopping by houses asking questions.

We had seen him stopping by Miss Clary's house, standing there smiling and talking to her. Inching down the sidewalk, he came right next door to Uncle's house standing there friendly and talking to him as he sat on his porch. Next, it was our turn to be friendly and smile at the man and talk with him in our yard.

"I need to ask y'all some questions, ok?"

"OK' we said in unison. Most answers are in unison.

Him: Do you live here?

Us: Yes

Him: Anybody home with you?

Us: Yes, we can get her.

Him: 'No that is ok. I think between the two of you I can get the right answers."

Do you live with Mom and Dad?

Us: Yes.

Him: Do you know how old your dad is?

Us: No.

Him: Do you think he is about thirty-five?

Us: We looked at each other and answered, 'Yes' because it sounded incredibly old, but we had no idea of his age.

Moun' Bah 'oh

Him: Do you know how old your mother is?

Us: In unison: Yes, sweet sixteen. (She never strayed from that answer until she turned one hundred years old in Jan 2024)

Him: The man looked shaken and said "sixteen !?" and gasped! Your mother is sixteen?!

Us: Yes! (We responded with the utmost confidence.)

Him: So how old are you?

Me: Five.

Him: Ok and how old are you?

Brother: Five.

Him: So, you are twins!

Us: No.

But y'all are the exact same size.

Us: Yes.

Frustration has set into this young fella dressed in the suit.

Him: So, you are five, and you are also five and you are not twins?

Us: We are not twins (Being Irish twins we are the same age for two weeks until I get my new number).

Moun' Bah 'oh

Moun' Bah 'oh

The census taker caught us within those 2 weeks. Poor fella.

He was at a loss for words, struggling on how to make sense of what we were saying.

Him: Ok. Uh... Ok...your father is thirty-five. Your mother cannot be sixteen so we will say she is twenty-five.

as he writes on his clip board...'OK, and does anyone else live in the house?

Us: Yes. Allan is 7 uh, 8, uh 7.

He just was standing there shaking his head with his face looking concerned and turning rosy colors.

He was sweating a little, confused and at his wits end, but as I recall had enough information to write down about us.

We left Moun' Ba' oh', and the heart of the civil rights movement, and the civil health movement in the summer of 1970…. On our way to Grand Mommy's house in North Carolina. Pa was going back to school to get more diplomas and degrees and such.

But anyway, Mound Bayou was something special.

Moun' Bah 'oh

Made in the USA
Columbia, SC
07 January 2025

51306261R00052